BREAKING FREE
FROM FEAR

BREAKING FREE
FROM FEAR

by
Marilyn Hickey

HARRISON HOUSE
Tulsa, Oklahoma

Unless otherwise indicated, all Scripture quotations are taken from the *King James Version* of the Bible.

06 05 04 03   10 9 8 7 6 5 4 3

Breaking Free From Fear
ISBN 1-57794-516-6
Previously published as *Fear Free, Faith Filled*
(ISBN 0-89274-259-3)
Copyright © 1952, 2002 by Marilyn Hickey
P.O. Box 17340
Denver, CO 80217

Published by Harrison House, Inc.
P. 0. Box 35035
Tulsa, OK 74153

Contents

1. What is Fear? 1

2. Kinds of Fear 9

3. Freedom From Fear...................................29

4. Triumph Over Fear 41

5. Come Out of Fear 51

6. Restoration for You 63

Endnotes 80

1

What Is Fear?

But without faith it is impossible to please him.

Hebrews 11:16

Fear is the opposite of faith. We are either in faith or in fear; the two cannot exist in the same place at the same time. Fear is Satan's number one weapon against the Christian. Through the Word of God, you can banish fear from your life.

One Greek word for fear is *phobos*[1] and is the word from which we get our English word *phobia*. Fear is a phobia which becomes more intense as you think on it, feed on it, and become more involved in it.

Phobos means "dread, or terror."[2] A person who has a phobia tends to be nervous in his reactions. He dreads facing certain things and is terrified by the object of his fear or phobia.

Another Greek word for fear is *deilia*,[3] the fearfulness that the Apostle Paul speaks of in 2 Timothy 1:7 when he declares, "For God hath not given us the spirit of fear; but of power, and of love, and of a sound mind." This kind of fear is never used in a positive sense because it denotes cowardliness and timidity.

Yet another word for fear in Greek is *eulabeia*[4] which means "caution." It can also mean "reverence and awe." We use it when speaking of the fear that is in love in regard to the fear of our heavenly Father. We are cautious in the way we obey Him and in the way we do His work.

Have you ever felt yourself shaking inside because you were afraid of a certain situation? That kind of fear is *chared*,[5] which means "trembling with fear."

The best word of all that has to do with fear is *aphobos*.[6] This word means "without fear." One of the places it is found in the Bible is in Luke 1:74:

That he would grant unto us, that we being delivered out of the hand of our enemies might serve him without fear.

Aphobos implies "being without fear among the Lord's people as the Lord's servant." At times, we can be fearful of other Christians and their opinions of us. You can imagine all the opinions we get in the ministry about what we are supposed to do and not do.

People frequently "feel led" to tell me what I should do in a particular situation. Sometimes there will be fifteen such opinions offered to me—all different and all "from the Lord." You have to reach the place that your priorities follow the Lord and His Word, regardless of whether or not you please other people.

If you are a leader of a Sunday School class or some other group, you must follow Jesus and stand uncompromisingly on God's Word. If you get involved in what other Christians think, it can lead to problems.

Years ago, a young girl in our church died of leukemia. This was a shock because we had prayed and stood in faith for her healing. When she died, it was nerve-racking for all of us.

A woman from outside the church called every family in the church and said, "Now, if the pastors are really spiritual, they will go to the funeral and raise that girl from the dead. If they don't do this, you can see that they don't really believe the Word. But I'll be there, and I'll raise her from the dead."

This woman was not a member of any church and had a flaky background. Through her calls, she sowed discord in the church.

The night before the funeral, I had at least ten telephone calls. My husband was out of town and I was home alone. Each of the people who called told me that the Lord was supposedly telling them what my husband was to do at the funeral. I never heard so many different opinions in my life. I was afraid of what would happen at the funeral with all the confusion from the outside.

When my husband came home, I told him about all the phone calls I had received. As I related the story to him, I became very distraught.

"What's wrong with you?" he asked. "We're looking to God. Lots of unsaved young people will attend that funeral tomorrow, and I'm claiming souls for Jesus. There's not going to be any confusion because we're taking power and authority over the devil tonight. He isn't going to do anything."

Later, that woman even got in touch with the family of the girl while they were in great grief and distress. She tried to cause some confusion with them the morning of the funeral.

My husband Wally met her outside the church and told her, "If you come in and try anything out of line, I'll have the police here to sit you down."

If we had looked at all the circumstances, we would have been afraid of Christians, but we took power and authority over the enemy and went to the funeral. The anointing of God moved in that service. Many young people indicated that they had received Jesus Christ as their personal Savior. We can always minister without fearing the opinions of others if we move in the Word.

There is another Scripture in which the word *aphobos* is used:

And many of the brethren in the Lord, waxing confident by my bonds, are much more bold to speak the word without fear.

Philippians 1:14

This means that you do not need to be afraid of how a person will react when you teach or minister the Word, or share it on a personal basis. You can have confidence that the Word will not return void. (Is. 55:11.) It will come to pass.

Once when I was teaching a group of Mormons, the enemy tried to put fear on me. I wasn't so afraid of the Mormons as I was concerned that they wouldn't receive the Word. The last morning of the retreat they all prayed the sinner's prayer and accepted the Lord Jesus Christ.

Immediately, the enemy said to me, "Yes, but they probably didn't mean it. You just gave them a high-powered sales job, and they did it to please you."

When I was teaching in Duluth, a couple came up to me the last Sunday night I was there and said, "Marilyn, we are Mormons. A very good friend of ours who was at the Mormon retreat told us of the changes in the women's lives after they prayed with you."

Isn't it good that God lets us hear some of these things? It makes us want to slap the devil in the face.

Jude 12 tells us not to be afraid of evil or false shepherds. The devil will recount to you such stories as that of the People's Temple in Guyana, South America. Evil spirits deceived the members of that group into taking their own lives under the leadership of the false shepherd, Jim Jones. You can understand how the enemy will try to strike fear in you by saying, "You know, you could get off into something false and evil." Remember, God says that we are not to be afraid of false or evil shepherds. God can, and will, deal with them.

An excellent Scripture in Proverbs tells us how to keep ourselves free from fear: "Whoso hearkeneth unto me shall dwell safely, and shall be quiet from fear of evil" (Prov. 1:33).

If you will hear God's Word, the Word is His voice, and listen to what God is saying, you will be free from the fear of evil and will dwell in a safe place. If your ears are tuned to the Word, that keeps you out of the realm of fear. I don't mean reading the Word a couple of times a week, but feeding on it every day. It will bring peace to your spirit.

2

Kinds of Fear

Let's examine the Old Testament definition of fear. Basically it comes from the Hebrew word *pachadh*, which means "terror," or "dread."[1] It can be used in referring to fear as being a companion for life.

The Bible says that we were under the bondage of fear (particularly the fear of death) all our lives: "And deliver them who through fear of death were all their lifetime subject to bondage" (Heb. 2:15).

Hebrews 2:15 says that all your life you had fear as a companion until you came to Jesus and let Him set you free from this lifelong companion.

Jesus said it was the fear of death. Jesus knew this was the lifetime companion of bondage.

There is a natural fear born in babies. As our children grow up, we feed them more fear by saying things like, "Be careful, honey, you're going to fall," or, "Don't cross the street alone; a car might run over you. Be sure to watch out for cars."

When they begin school, we say, "Now, the first day may really be hard on you. The kids may not like you. Someone may knock you down, but you will be all right." We begin to build on that inborn fear and help it to develop. I don't care to have that kind of life-time companion.

Following are five examples from the Word of God which show how Jesus dealt with five entirely different types of fear. The first account is in Matthew 9:2:

And behold, they brought to him a man sick of the palsy, lying on a bed: and Jesus seeing

their faith said unto the sick of the palsy; Son, be of good cheer; thy sins be forgiven thee.

Examine that verse very closely. Notice the pronoun *their*. In giving this account, the other Gospels reveal that because Jesus was in a very crowded house, and because it was extremely difficult for the friends of the man to get to Him, they actually cut a hole in the roof and let him down into the presence of Jesus so he could receive healing.

The man was sick of the palsy which is a disease that causes various degrees of shaking and involuntary trembling. Remember, one of the meanings of fear is shaking and trembling.

I think palsy can be caused by fear. Look at what Jesus said to this poor man who, shaking and helpless, was in such a bad state when let down through that hole in the roof. The Word says that Jesus saw the faith of the men who had brought the palsied man. He saw *their* faith. This

11

shows how we can have faith for people who are in fear.

Sometimes we say, "If that person just had faith, he wouldn't be in that condition." I hate to hear that statement come out of the mouth of a Christian. If that person doesn't have faith, *you* need to have faith for him. You have a responsibility.

Notice the term Jesus used when He spoke to the sick man. He didn't just say, "Be of good cheer; thy sins are forgiven thee." He said, **Son,** *be of good cheer....* That is important.

If you are struggling through a time of depression, and someone comes to you and says, "Oh, snap out of it. Be cheerful. Don't be like that." You might be able to try that for a few minutes, but you won't keep it up for very long.

Every time Jesus speaks the word *cheer,* He dealt with fear. Here in Matthew, cheer means "courage." When Jesus called the man, *Son,* He also said, *Thy sins be forgiven thee.* That man's sins had made him shaky, fearful, and trembling. He was literally scared to death because he was a sinner. He was afraid of God.

When Jesus said, *Son,* He was saying, "Relax. You're in the family. God's not mad at you. He loves you." Jesus stepped into the situation and stood between the man and his fear of God by saying, "Don't worry, Son; your sins are forgiven."

The other men around Jesus at the time got very upset over this.

> And, behold, certain of the scribes said within themselves, This man blasphemeth.
>
> And Jesus knowing their thoughts said, Wherefore think ye evil in your hearts?
>
> For whether is easier, to say, Thy sins be forgiven thee; or to say, Arise, and walk?
>
> But that ye may know that the Son of man hath power on earth to forgive sins, (then saith he to the sick of the palsy,) Arise, take up thy bed, and go unto thine house.
>
> **Matthew 9:3-6**

When this man was set free from his sins, he was set free from fear. When he was set free from fear, he was set free from sickness. See the pattern?

Sin is not always the cause of every sickness, but in this situation, it was. Jesus said, "Be of good courage." The man was healed from sin, healed from fear, and healed from sickness.

The next example is found in Matthew 9:22:

Jesus turned him about, and when he saw her, he said, Daughter, be of good comfort; thy faith hath made thee whole. And the woman was made whole from that hour.

The woman mentioned here had an issue of blood for twelve years. When she touched the hem of Jesus' garment, she was healed.

Jesus was on His way to heal the daughter of Jairus, the ruler of the synagogue. The girl was only twelve years old and was about to die. It is interesting that this account is about two women; one was twelve years old and near death, the other had been sick for twelve years. Each received a miracle.

In both instances, faith was involved in order for Jesus to move. The woman who had been ill for twelve years said to herself, *If I may but touch his garment, I shall be whole* (v. 21).

In Mark 11:23 Jesus said, "Whosoever shall say unto this mountain, Be thou removed, and be thou cast into the sea; and shall not doubt in his heart, but shall believe that those things which he saith shall come to pass; he shall have whatsoever he saith."

The woman *said*, "If I touch His garment, I'll be whole." She would be whole if she touched His garment because she *said* it.

This woman was sneaky about what she was doing because Leviticus tells us a woman with an issue of blood was not allowed to go into the synagogue or into the temple. She was not allowed to visit anyone's house. In fact, if the ailment didn't stop, her husband was to leave her. She was an outcast from home and society. She couldn't work for anyone because she was considered unclean.

This explains why this woman was afraid to touch Jesus or even to let Him know what she was going to do. She had a fear; she was afraid of people.

You have to admire her. She did have enough boldness to say to herself, "If I can just touch His garment, I shall be whole," and then to do it.

In more than one place in the Bible we read about the hem of a person's garment. At the hem there was a little blue thread design sewn with tassels. That blue thread was a sign that the person was obedient to the Word of God and dedicated to following it. When that woman reached through and touched the hem of Jesus' garment, she was touched by the Living Word.

Jesus immediately said, "Who touched my clothes?" (Mark 5:30). Jesus and His disciples were probably moving along at a rapid pace through a throng of people. The disciples thought, *We're in a crowd and everybody is touching Him.* Jesus said to Himself, *Virtue has gone out of Me.* (v. 30.) "Virtue" here means "miracle-working power." The Greek word for it *is dunamis.*[2]

In speaking the Word, you release the *dunamis* power of God. People say, "Oh, if only I had miracle-working power. I want that kind of power." Jesus told His disciples, if you will tarry in Jerusalem, you'll be endued with power from on high. (Acts 1:8.) That's *dunamis* power. Spirit-filled people have God's miracle-working power. We don't see more Spirit-filled Christians moving in God's miracle-working power because it takes the Word to release that power.

There are two kinds of power: *exousia,*[3] or authority power, and *dunamis,* or miracle-working power. Jesus used this latter word when He said, "Ye do err, not knowing the scriptures, nor the power (dunamis) *of God*" (Matt. 22:29).

Jesus was saying, *The Scriptures give you the authority power. If you don't know the Word, you can't be full in the flow of God.* This describes the basic difference between the fundamentalists and the Spirit-filled people. The fundamentalists are heavy on *knowing* the Word. The Spirit-filled people can be weak knowing the Word, but heavy on *using* the power of the Word. One group denies the power, but believes Word. The other group believes in the power, but lacks in knowledge of the Word. If you are going to be balanced, you must have the Word *and* the power.

After the woman who touched Jesus' garment was healed, she was afraid. Jesus turned to her and said, "Daughter, be of good comfort; thy faith hath made thee whole" (v 22).

If you're a sinner, you don't have to be afraid of God. God loves you. Jesus didn't say to the woman, "You outcast. You unclean thing." Instead, He made her whole—spiritually, mentally, emotionally, and physically. He brought her back into society and made her a somebody. Jesus wants to turn "nobodies" into "somebodies."

This woman not only feared people, God, and her own physical illness, she was probably also afraid because of her poor finances. Another verse tells us that she had spent everything she had for cures, but didn't get any better, only worse. She was probably fearful that, if something didn't happen soon, she would starve. Jesus knew she was in fear. To release her from all her fears, He told her, "Be of good comfort" (v 22).

Jesus is saying the same thing to you today to release you from all your fears: "Be of good cheer." You'll see that He wants, "Be of good cheer," to be a divine order for your life.

Let's look at another time Jesus used this same phrase. In Matthew 14 we read where Jesus went up into a mountain to pray. He sent His disciples away, telling them to get into a ship and go to the other side of the lake.

And straightway Jesus constrained his disciples to get into a ship, and to go before him unto the other side, while he sent the multitudes away.

And when he had sent the multitudes away, he went up into a mountain apart to pray: and when the evening was come, he was there alone.

But the ship was now in the midst of the sea, tossed with waves: for the wind was contrary.

And in the fourth watch of the night Jesus went unto them, walking on the sea.

Matthew 14:22

Jesus actually saw the disciples out on the lake. (Mark 6:48.) Think about the timing of *when* Jesus saw them. He was on a mountain praying. It was dark. That little ship was in the middle of the sea and the storm and the wind had surrounded them. They were not out of the will of God because Jesus had told them to cross over.

If the Lord told you to cross the sea during a storm, you might wonder about His reasoning, but you would still obey, wouldn't you? If there is a storm, He will take you across. He spoke the Word; therefore, we know we're going to get across.

Jesus was on the mountain, watching the disciples toil at sea. If you have ever been to that area, you know that in the natural you can't see out on the Sea of Galilee at night. It's impossible because it gets so dark there. Actually, even in the daylight you can't see very well. From a mountain you might be able to see that it is windy, or that a storm is raging because the waves are high, but to see a boat would be very difficult, even in daylight. At night, it would be impossible.

Jesus must have "seen" the disciples by the Spirit. He saw them there out in the dark, rowing and rowing with all their might in the raging storm. He followed them with His spiritual eye. Before too long, He went out to the boat walking on the water. When the disciples saw Him, they were frightened. At first, they thought He was a spirit or a ghost. As He neared the ship, He said, "It is I; be not afraid" (John 6:20).

Sometimes when we begin to do something and an unusual event occurs in the process of our task, we become afraid. We think, *I know Jesus told me to do this, but the storm looks bad. I'm afraid of what's going to happen.* We are afraid of the unknown. But then Jesus comes walking by. He knows we are afraid.

Sometimes people are afraid of Word-based spiritual experiences. A woman once said to me, "Marilyn, I'm afraid of getting the baptism in the Holy Spirit. When you speak in tongues, does the power come over you so that you can't control yourself anymore? I see people raising their hands and getting very emotional. I don't want to be emotional. Do I have to be so emotional to speak in tongues?"

The Spirit of God was unknown and mysterious to her and she was afraid of Him. I think Jesus wanted to say to her, "It is I, the Lord. You don't have to be afraid. I won't make you do anything unseemly." He doesn't make us do anything that does not glorify Him. When a Spirit-filled Christian does something wrong, he is just acting in the flesh. Just because someone else wrecks his brand-new car doesn't keep me from buying a new one.

When the Lord comes to you in a beautiful new way, let Him employ His variety. Don't insist on Him being the same way every time. It can be different and still be Jesus.

He sees you when you are in those dark times, when it looks like you don't know where you are going. You may be obeying His Word, yet you're rowing and rowing, seemingly getting no place. The winds are contrary and everything is coming against you. But Jesus sees you, and He will meet you there. He won't leave you or forsake you.

And when the disciples saw him walking on the sea, they were troubled, saying, It is a spirit, and they cried out for fear.

But straightway Jesus spake unto them, saying, Be of good cheer; it is I; be not afraid.

And Peter answered him and said, Lord, if it be thou, bid me come unto thee on the water.

Matthew 14:26-28

Impetuous Peter. He wanted to walk on the water with Jesus, but he knew he had to have the Word before he could do it.

Jesus said, "Come" (v. 29).

Peter began walking, then started looking at the wind and the waves. Verse 30 says, "But when he saw the wind boisterous, he was afraid; and beginning to sink, he cried, saying, Lord, save me."

Now here is a very unusual expression: "Beginning to sink." Have you ever "begun" to sink? When you dive into the water, do you "begin" to go into the water and "begin" to sink? No, once you hit the water, you're in.

Peter didn't sink instantly; he started to sink a little bit at a time. Whenever we begin to look at circumstances, we start slipping in our faith. We may not go under immediately, but we "begin to sink" a little.

As soon as Peter began to sink, he cried out to Jesus. Jesus instantly reached out to him, and they both walked back to the ship.

In these accounts of Matthew and John, Jesus said, "It is I; be not afraid." This is the same as saying, "Be of good cheer. Be of good courage. I am here. I'll take care of you." Whenever we face the mysterious and become afraid, Jesus says, "I'm here. I'll move into the situation. You don't have to be afraid."

Another example of "good cheer" is found in the book of Acts:

And the night following the Lord stood by him, and said, Be of good cheer, Paul: for as thou hast testified of me in Jerusalem, so must thou bear witness also at Rome.

Acts 23:11

Paul was frightened; a mob was out to kill him. Everybody was yelling, screaming, and carrying on. Paul escaped by the skin of his teeth.

Jesus had told him that he was supposed to go to Rome and bring them the Word, but it didn't look like he was going to make it. I think Paul was afraid that his life would be cut short before he got to Rome and that he wouldn't be able to fulfill God's call on his life.

The Lord stood by Paul's side and told him, "Be of good cheer, Paul." That's not like saying, "Cheer up; put a smile on your face." Jesus was saying, "Be of good courage, Paul, for whereas you have testified of Me in Jerusalem, so must you bear witness of Me also in Rome. I'll get you there."

When Jesus told Paul to go to Rome, that didn't mean that Paul would have no problems. He had a few—even a shipwreck.

You must stand and keep looking at God's Word until the storm passes.

Another time Jesus said, "Be of good cheer," applies directly to you and me.

These things I have spoken unto you, that in me ye might have peace. In the world ye shall have tribulation: but be of good cheer; I have overcome the world.

John 16:31

Jesus was talking to the disciples. They knew that He was supposed to be King and Messiah, but everything was falling apart around them. Things looked bad.

Jesus had said to them, "Behold, the hour cometh, yea, is now come, that ye shall be scattered, every man to his own, and shall leave me alone: and yet I am not alone, because the Father is with me" (v. 32).

The disciples were afraid of what the world would do to them. If you are ever afraid of what the world can do to you and your loved ones, remember that Jesus has left His peace for you to dwell in. Jesus has overcome the world and you can too. Greater is He Who is in you than he who is in the world. (1 John 4:4.)

3

Freedom From Fear

To the man who was sick of the palsy, Jesus said, "Son, be of good cheer; your sins are forgiven." In the process of having his sins forgiven, the man was freed from fear.

Even though the man was released from fear, the crowd was filled with fear: "And they were all amazed, and they glorified God, and were filled with fear" (Luke 5:26). The man who was freed from fear took Jesus into his situation.

The woman, outcast because of her health, went to Jesus even though she was afraid to approach Him face to face. She had faith. She said, "If I can but touch the hem of His garment, I'll be made whole." She was afraid of being pushed out of the way, and also afraid that Jesus might reject her. She acted in faith and received *dunamis,* the miracle-working power of God, to make her whole.

An important thing to realize concerning fear is that you can quote Scriptures against fear all day long, yet remain in fear. I speak Isaiah 54:14 again and again: "Fear and oppression are far from me." Fear is oppression. According to the Bible, it is a bondage. Sometimes I don't *feel* like fear is far from me.

Besides confessing the Word, we need to catch a vision of Jesus. We need to see Him between us and the fear. Confess the Word and see Jesus in your situation, standing between you and whatever it is that is trying to attach itself to you.

Jesus spoke to the disciples on the storm-tossed sea and said, "It is I. Don't be afraid." They were afraid until they saw Jesus. When they saw Jesus, fear left.

The disciples in the upper room were afraid of what the world would do to them. Nobody knew what was going to happen. Jesus told them that He was going to die. But He said, "Don't be afraid. Look at Me. I've overcome the world. I will stand between you and every attack that the world makes against you."

What the world brings along doesn't matter. Get a vision of Jesus standing between you and the problem situation. That's what makes the difference.

Some years ago, when the atheists attacked my television broadcast—a Bible program on educational TV—I could see Jesus standing between the atheists and the TV program. I knew He was there because He said, "I have overcome the world." I didn't have to be afraid of what the world was going to try to do because Jesus has already overcome the world. When the atheistic woman who led the campaign against me went before the TV committee to have my program thrown off the air, they threw her out instead.

The only times recorded in the Bible that Jesus said, "Be of good cheer," are contained in the four examples above. I believe these parallel the four occasions that all mankind faces. When God tells you to do something, but all surrounding evidence makes it look like you can't (as happened with Paul), the Lord will come to help. The people in all these examples saw Jesus.

See Jesus in your situation. Confess the Word and have a vision of Jesus standing between you and that which you fear. Remember, the Bible says that without a vision, the people perish. (Prov. 29:18.)

Once I had an invitation to speak at a charismatic conference of Lutherans. The man in charge disliked women teachers. In fact, one time he had told his church, "Don't read any of Marilyn Hickey's books. She is a false prophetess. Don't listen to her on radio and don't watch her telecast because she is wrong. As a woman, she should not be a teacher."

You can imagine my surprise when later a woman from that conference called me to ask, "Would you be a teacher at our conference?"

I thought, *I must be dreaming. That man is head of this conference and here I am being invited to speak there.*

"Do you know whom you are calling?" I asked the lady.

"Isn't your name Marilyn Hickey?"

"Yes."

"Can't you do it?"

"My calendar will allow it, but I just can't imagine you inviting me."

I had such a witness that I was supposed to go that I said, "Yes, I can do it." When I hung up the phone, I leaned against the wall and said, "Lord, what are You doing?"

Suddenly, I was flooded with fear. I thought, *Is that man inviting me so he can put me on a platform before all those thousands of people and say, "Here is a false prophetess"?* Fear rolled over me.

Then the Holy Spirit said to me, "Marilyn, when I open doors before you, no man can close them. When men open doors before you that are not of Me, I will close them."

When it came time for me to speak at the conference, I had to sit next to that man. Besides that, I was the only woman on the platform. I thought, *He's probably thinking, "I have to sit by you."* But God said to me, "Stop thinking that way. Hold your peace, and I'll take care of your enemies. Just be quiet."

We are to love our enemies, do good to them, pray for them, and bless them. I tried to do all the nice things I could think of for that pastor. Eventually, God turned that man's attitude around so much so that he later invited me to speak four different times in his church.

We have victory over all the different kinds of fear by speaking faith words and seeing Jesus standing between us and the things we fear.

THE FEAR OF DEATH

Hebrews 2:15 says, "And deliver them who through fear of death were all their lifetime subject to bondage."

"Christians shouldn't be afraid of death," you may say.

That's true, but the fact is that many people are afraid of dying. It is not enough to tell them, "Oh, don't be like that." That is no answer to their fear.

Instead, we need to tell such people, "Jesus will make you free of fear because He has come between you and death. He tasted death for every man. You don't have to be afraid of death because Jesus conquered it. Get a vision of Jesus standing between you and death."

Paul said, "To die is gain" (Phil. 1:21). Why? Because when we die we go to be with Jesus.

THE FEAR OF EVIL

This is a terribly evil day in which we live. All kinds of evil things happen: rapes, burglaries, kidnappings, murders, plane crashes, car wrecks. Because we are continually hearing such bad news, we can be hit hard by the fear of evil. But according to Proverbs 1:33, "Whoso hearkeneth unto me shall dwell safely, and shall be quiet from fear of evil."

The Bible says that in these last days men's hearts will fail them for fear. Did you know that doctors say that eighty percent of all illness is caused by fear?

Christians have fears, even those in the faith walk. Though Christians confess the Word, fear can still hang around. Perhaps this occurs because the Christian has no vision of Jesus to go along with his confession.

Jesus is the Word. When you confess Scriptures toward your situation, see Jesus in your mind's eye. When the disciples saw Jesus, they weren't afraid any longer. By speaking the Word and seeing Jesus, your fears will leave too.

THE FEAR OF WAR

Psalm 27:3 says, "Though an host should encamp against me, my heart shall not fear: though war should rise against me, in this will I be confident."

We don't need to be afraid of the threat of war—we have a vision of Jesus. We're trusting in Him.

THE FEAR OF EVIL TIDINGS

Whenever I'm on a trip, the devil really tries to chew on me before I call home. He will say, "What if you call home and find out your daughter has been hurt? Or your son has been in an accident? Or your church has burned down? You're going to hear something bad when you call."

Psalm 112:7 is the answer to such fears: "He (the faithful man) shall not be afraid of evil tidings: his heart is fixed, trusting in the Lord."

THE FEAR OF MAN

Proverbs 29:25 states, "The fear of man bringeth a snare." The following Scriptures give the antidote to that fear:

I, even I, am he that comforteth you: who art thou, that thou shouldest be afraid of a man that shall die, and of the son of man which shall be made as grass;

And forgettest the Lord thy maker, that hath stretched forth the heavens, and laid the foundations of the earth; and hast feared continually every day because of the fury of the oppressor, as if he were ready to destroy? and where is the fury of the oppressor?

Isaiah 51:12,13

"Where is the fury of the oppressor?" Why are you afraid of man, anyway? Man will die and pass away like the grass, but Jesus will be around to hold you up forever. Never be afraid of people.

When you see someone who is afraid, be an encouragement to him. Instead of saying, "Too bad. You didn't make your faith confession every day," go to him and love him. Stand in faith for him.

I want to emphasize one more point regarding the man who was sick with the palsy.

When the man's friends brought him to Jesus, he was so afraid that he was shaking. One of the meanings of fear is "to shake." His friends didn't say to him, "Well, if you hadn't been such a sinner, you wouldn't be in this state. You need to repent."

Faith doesn't work that way. Faith works by love. We have no business deciding who has faith and who doesn't. If we know that a certain person is weak in faith, we need to have faith for him.

The Bible says, "Jesus saw their faith." Notice what the Scriptures say about the strength of combined faith: "How should one chase a thousand, and two put ten thousand to flight" (Deut. 32:30).

When two or more believers put their faith together, they can chase ten thousand. Let's quit criticizing others who have fears as we do, and get busy chasing demons. None of us is as high in faith as he should be. We should see the good in everyone. If we can't see faith in another person, we should pray that he too will be brought into the great place of faith and power which we enjoy.

When we walk in faith, we don't criticize because faith works by love. If we're not moving in love, we're not moving in faith. We can't please God without faith, and faith won't work without love. They go together.

We should quit criticizing, unite our faith, start confessing the Word for others, and loving them. When we do, we will bring them into a place of faith they have never been before.

4

Triumph Over Fear

Often, fear doesn't leave overnight. One day it may not bother us; the next day it may hit us hard. Fear tends to have a pattern to it.

Let's examine the life of Peter to see where fear took him and how Jesus restored him. By studying the restoration process of Jesus, we can learn how to be free from the cycle of fear.

The first step in overcoming fear is to rebuke it the very moment it comes to us. If we entertain it, it will move in and take over the imagination.

PETER'S PROFESSION

Peter said to Jesus, "Thou art the Christ, the Son of the living God" (Matt. 16:16).

That was a marvelous thing for Peter to say. Jesus was really complimented. In return, Jesus said to Peter:

Blessed art thou, Simon Bar-jona: flesh and blood hath not revealed it unto thee, but my Father which is in heaven.

And I say also unto thee, That thou art Peter, and upon this rock I will build my church; and the gates of hell shall not prevail against it.

Matthew 16:17,18

Peter had made a tremendous statement to Jesus: "You are the Son of God." In response, Jesus said, "You didn't get this from flesh and blood. This is a revelation of the Spirit, and on this statement I will build My Church."

The Church is built, not on Peter, but on his statement, "Thou art the Christ, the Son of the living God." The Church of Jesus Christ is not built on a man, but on the fact that Jesus is the Son of God.

Just a few short months after making the greatest statement of the whole New Testament, Peter made the worst one. He denied that he had ever known the man, Jesus of Nazareth. How could one person be so extreme? One time he spoke the best words; the next time, the worst.

Have you ever done anything like that? You confess the Word and have the greatest victories; then five hours later, you blow it. *Oh, God,* you think. *How did I ever do that?* Let's see why that happens so that you will know how to avoid it the next time.

PETER'S DENIAL

Then began he (Peter) to curse and to swear, saying, I know not the man.

Matthew 26:74

Peter, the same man who earlier had said, "Thou art the Christ, the Son of the living God," then proclaimed, "I don't know the man." He cursed and totally denied his Lord.

Peter denied Christ because he was afraid. Jesus had been taken prisoner, and Peter was afraid that he too would be thrown into prison. When the people said to him, "Hey, you run around with that Galilean, you know who He is," fear rose up in Peter, and he began to curse. He didn't want to be connected with Jesus because he was afraid he too would be crucified. Out of fear, Peter denied the Lord.

Most of our wrong statements are made out of fear. When fear comes in, it makes things seem like a mountain. As a result, we make wrong statements.

Most of the time, we don't jump into things. Usually it is a long gradual process that brings us into something good or bad. It's like when we first began to read the Word; we learned precept upon precept, line upon line. (Is. 28:13.)

Building faith is like building character. It is a process. We go from faith to faith, strength to strength, glory to glory. We confess Jesus as our Lord and Savior. That's the first confession, the great confession. As we walk with Him, we begin to learn the Word, confess the Word, and go into higher levels of faith. Faithfulness isn't arrived at overnight.

Mistakes and bad statements are progressive in the same way. They start with one negative thing. If we keep feeding that kind of situation by speaking bad words over it, we begin to go down and down and down. Let's look at Peter's life to find out where he began this process.

After making the tremendous statement, "You are the Christ, the Son of the Living God," Peter got into some trouble. He made a very bad statement. It came right out of his heart, but it was sincerely wrong.

Some people today have lifted up sincerity and said, "If people are sincere, that's all that matters." That's not true. Sincerity is not the answer. We must be sincere about the right thing.

Jesus told His disciples that He was going to die on the cross and be resurrected. When Peter heard this, he began to go wrong:

> **Then Peter took him, and began to rebuke him, saying, Be it far from thee, Lord: this shall not be unto thee.**
>
> **Matthew 16:2**

Peter was bold. He made the above statement right after he had confessed Jesus as the Christ. The response Jesus made to Peter shows us that the Church wasn't built upon Peter, but upon his confession of Christ as the Son of God:

> **He (Jesus) turned, and said unto Peter, Get thee behind me, Satan: thou art an offence unto me: for thou savourest not the things that be of God, but those that be of men.**
>
> **Matthew 16:2**

Just six verses earlier Jesus had praised Peter and called him "blessed." Now He is rebuking him and addressing him as "Satan." Peter's first mistake was in trying to say that the cross was wrong.

You may say, "He did it out of compassion for Jesus." I don't think so. I think the reason, once again, was fear. Peter was saying, "We've found the Messiah. He's the Son of God. He's going to take us out of Roman rule. He's going to sit on a throne, and we're going to be right beside Him to rule and reign with Him."

Peter failed to see that before the crown came the cross. When Jesus mentioned the cross, Peter thought that did away with the throne. Fear struck Peter and he said, "Oh, no. I won't let You do that." Peter's first area of fear was fear of the cross.

Our human personalities make us afraid to die to our own desires. We're afraid to say, "Okay, Jesus, I'm willing to surrender all to You." Paul said, "I am crucified with Christ: nevertheless I live; yet not I, but Christ liveth in me" (Gal. 2:20).

We need to be willing to crucify many of our wrong desires. Sometimes we have a fear about what this means, or we want to clutch little things to ourselves. Peter was afraid of the cross. Once that fear crept in, other negative things followed.

Peter began to say things that were not good. (Matt. 26:31-35.) He began to boast, not in the Word, but in himself. The Bible says that we are not to have confidence in the flesh, but rather to have confidence in the Word. If we start boasting in our own strength, having confidence in the flesh, we will get into trouble every time. The following passage reveals Peter's confidence in his own strength:

> **Then saith Jesus unto them, All ye shall be offended because of me this night: for it is written, I will smite the shepherd, and the sheep of the flock shall be scattered abroad.**
>
> **But after I am risen again, I will go before you in Galilee.**
>
> **Peter answered and said unto him, Though all men shall be offended because of thee, yet will I never be offended.**

Jesus said unto him, Verily I say unto thee, That this night, before the cock crow, thou shalt deny me thrice.

Peter said unto him, Though I should die with thee, yet will I not deny thee.

Matthew 26:31-35

"I would never do that," Peter boasted. Christians sometimes talk about others, saying, "Have you heard about so-and-so? He really blew it. I can't understand why he would do something like that. I would never do that." People who say such things have confidence in the flesh.

We can say, "Jesus in me is greater than he who is in the world, and I can do all things through Christ Who strengthens me." Having confidence in the Word will take us through.

Peter had confidence in himself, not in the Word. Fear may take us to the point of saying, "I'm going to be brave." But we're still putting confidence in the wrong thing. Peter wanted to be brave, but put confidence in himself.

When the soldiers came for Jesus, Peter, in his zeal to protect Jesus, took his sword and cut off the ear of the High Priest's servant. (Mark 14:47.) Peter was trying to keep Jesus from going to the cross because he was afraid of it. In Mark 14:53,54 we learn of something else that fear did to Peter:

And they led Jesus away to the high priest: and with him were assembled all the chief priests and the elders and the scribes.

And Peter followed him afar off ....

Fear will keep us from trusting Jesus; it will cause us to put a distance between us and Him. You may be following Him, but that distance appears because fear doesn't please God. It is faith that pleases God.

5

Come Out of Fear

Fear is the opposite of faith. Peter began to follow Jesus from a distance the first time he told Jesus, "I'll never let You go to the cross. I'll die before I let You do that." Peter's words put him in a position of following afar off.

> And as Peter was beneath in the palace, there cometh one of the maids of the high priest: and when she saw Peter warming himself, she looked upon him, and said, And thou also wast with Jesus of Nazareth.

> But he denied, saying, I know not, neither understand I what thou sayest. And he went out into the porch; and the cock crew.

And a maid saw him again, and began to say to them that stood by, This is one of them.

And he denied it again. And a little after, they that stood by said again to Peter, Surely thou art one of them: for thou art a Galilean, and thy speech agreeth thereto.

But he began to curse and to swear, saying, I know not this man of whom ye speak.

And the second time the cock crew. And Peter called to mind the word that Jesus said unto him, Before the cock crow twice, thou shalt deny me thrice. And when he though thereon, he wept.

Mark 14:66-72

Peter felt condemned by what he had done because he knew he had acted out of fear. Excusing our false actions by saying, "I did it because I was afraid," doesn't make them right.

Initially, Peter was afraid of the cross. From there his fear grew. He was afraid he was going to have to go to the cross with Jesus, that he might have to die there. His "following afar off" and his denial of Jesus started with fear. Peter should have taken the word of Jesus; instead, Jesus had to tell him, "Get behind Me, Satan. You don't savor the things of God."

The cross is a place of victory, not of defeat. Peter took several steps away from victory, all because of fear.

Following the steps that brought Peter out of fear will also bring us out of fear. We need to start every day with the confession: "Fear and oppression are far from me." (Is. 54:14.) We can avoid being attacked by fear by beginning the day this way.

Fear can be a devilish, hideous thing. The Bible says "fear and oppression" because fear is oppressive; it is an ugly thing. One of the first statements Adam made was in response to God's question as to why he was hiding. Adam said, "I was afraid." (Gen. 3:10.) He was hiding from God. His fear separated him from God.

God is looking for people who are afraid so that He can bring them out of their fear. That is why there is a plan to set people free from fear.

Let's look at the steps that brought Peter out of fear:

STEP ONE: HOLD ON TO JESUS

And the Lord said, Simon, Simon, behold, Satan hath desired to have you, that he may sift you as wheat: But I have prayed for thee, that thy faith fail not: and when thou art converted, strengthen thy brethren.

Luke 22:31,32

Jesus called Peter "Simon" on some occasions and "Peter" the rest of the time. Peter is the name Jesus used originally. Simon means "hearing." The first time Jesus called Peter "Simon Bar-jona," He was saying, "Simon, you are a hearing one." When Peter said to Jesus, "Thou art the Christ, the Son of the living God," Jesus answered, "Simon, flesh and blood didn't reveal this to you. You've been hearing it from the Spirit."

In Luke 22:31,32 Jesus says, "Simon, you've been a hearing one. Satan is going to try to sift you, but I have prayed for you that your faith won't fail. When you are converted, you're going to strengthen the brethren."

Peter responds, "Lord, I am ready to go with thee, both into prison, and to death" (v. 33).

Jesus answers, "I tell thee, Peter, the cock shall not crow this day, before that thou shalt thrice deny that thou knowest me" (v. 34).

As Jesus said, Peter's faith did not fail, even though his courage did. He did many stupid things, but his faith didn't fail; he went out and wept still believing in Jesus.

Sometimes when we say the wrong things, we feel like we have failed because, after confessing faith, we got into a fear level. Then we say, "I've just blown it. There's no use trying again." This is not true. Just hang in there with Jesus and say, "I still believe You. I may have blown it, I may have said and done all the wrong things, but somehow I'm still holding on to You." Your courage may fail, but your faith won't.

Jesus said to Peter, "I have prayed for you." The Bible tells us Jesus prays for us. Hebrews 7:25 says that Jesus, seated at the right hand of the Father, ever lives to make intercession for us.

The first step in getting rid of fear is to remember that Jesus is praying for you. When you are afraid, think, *Satan is trying to sift me, but Jesus is praying for me.*

The Bible tells us in Luke 22 that while Peter was denying Jesus, Jesus heard him:

But a certain maid beheld him (Peter) as he sat by the fire, and earnestly looked upon him, and said, This man was also with him.

And he denied him, saying, Woman, I know him not.

And after a little while another saw him, and said, Thou art also of them. And Peter said, Man, I am not.

And about the space of one hour after, another confidently affirmed, saying, Of a truth this fellow also was with him: for he is a Galilean.

And Peter said, Man, I know not what thou sayest. And immediately, while he yet spake, the cock crew.

And (then) the Lord turned, and looked upon Peter....

Luke 22:56-61

The verb translated here "looked upon" doesn't mean "to look at," it means "to look through." Jesus looked through Peter. I believe it said, "Peter, don't do this to yourself."

STEP TWO: TRUST JESUS

The second step in getting rid of fear is to know that Jesus sees us. He sees us right where we are, just as we are. And He loves us as we are, even when we feel that we have let Him and everyone else down. Without condemning us, He looks through us to help us make it.

After the Resurrection, the Bible tells us that Jesus came to His disciples. Remember, the last look that Peter had from Jesus was while he was denying Him. Now Jesus has risen from the dead. Notice what the angels say in the following passage:

And when the sabbath was past, Mary Magdalene, and Mary the mother of James, and Salome, had bought sweet spices, that they might come and anoint him.

And very early in the morning the first day of the week, they came unto the sepulchre at the rising the sun.

And they said among themselves, Who shall roll us away the stone from the door of the sepulchre?

And when they looked, they saw that the stone was rolled away: for it was very great.

And entering into the sepulchre, they saw a young man sitting on the right side, clothed in a long white garment; and they were affrighted.

And he saith unto them, Be not, affrighted: Ye seek Jesus of Nazareth, which was crucified: he is risen; he is not here: behold the place where they laid him.

But go your way, tell his disciples and Peter....

Mark 16:1-7

The angel didn't say, "Go tell His disciples." Jesus wanted Peter to have a personal message: "Peter, I'm not mad at you. I know you followed afar off. I know you got in your own zeal and cut off the ear of the priest's servant, and I had to do one of My last miracles because you blew it. I know you cursed. I know you denied Me, but, Peter, I want you to know that it was right for Me to go to the cross. I want you to know that I am risen."

When you've been in the midst of a real attack of fear, have you ever said, "God give me a Scripture"? Jesus will speak to you personally and give you one. Many times Jesus has impressed into my spirit a specific verse. His sheep know His voice.

One time I was undergoing a very difficult trial. The natural circumstances seemed to me almost unbearable. I said, "God, I must have something specific from the Word. I know all these Scriptures that I claim every day, but I must have something new."

God gave me a wonderful Scripture from Haggai. I had read this book many times without ever seeing this verse as a personal word to me. Whenever the devil tries to hit me with fear about this situation, I quote this verse:

> **According to the word that I covenanted with you when ye came out of Egypt, so my spirit remaineth among you: fear ye not.**
>
> **Haggai 2:5**

STEP THREE: LISTEN TO JESUS

The third step in the restoration process is to hear the personal message Jesus has for you.

Jesus not only sent a message to Peter, He also had a personal interview with him after the Resurrection. The Bible tells us in 1 Corinthians 15:5 "that he (Jesus) was seen of Cephas (Peter), then of the twelve."

John 20 gives the account of Jesus' appearance before the disciples in the room with all the doors locked. (v. 19.) But before He appeared in that room, Jesus had already appeared to Peter. He wanted to tell Peter that everything was okay.

At times, Jesus wants a personal interview with us. He just wants us to wait in His presence for Him to refresh us. He wants to say, "I'm with you personally."

Remember, Jesus said, "I will never leave thee nor forsake thee" (Heb. 13:5). People have had personal interviews with God many times. Wait in God's presence. He has personal time for you, too.

Some of us might say, "Jesus could have been angry with Peter; maybe that's the reason He wanted to meet with him in private." But Jesus isn't angry with people who are afraid. He is praying for them and trying to bring them out of their fear.

This is how we should be, too. We shouldn't become upset with people who are afraid. If we are in faith, we need to bring those people out of fear and into faith by lifting them up and giving them the Word.

6

Restoration for You

Jesus deals with Peter because Peter has been fearful and unbelieving. (John 21:15-22.) Someone might say, "Jesus still loves Peter." Yes, but Jesus had to deal with Peter right where he was, right where the stem of the fear was. Peter had to face his fear in order to be set free. Sympathy will never set us free from fear, but God's Word will.

After these things Jesus shewed himself again to the disciples at the sea of Tiberias; and on this wise shewed he himself. There were together Simon Peter, and Thomas called Didymus, and Nathanael of Cana in Galilee, and the sons of Zebedee, and two

other of his disciples. Simon Peter saith unto
them, I go a fishing.

John 21:1-3

In the Greek, Peter was actually saying "I'm
going back to the fishing trade." After Peter has
had a personal interview with Jesus, he's going
back to the fishing business because there's still
something about the cross that's bothering him.
Whenever a leader turns back, he always takes
some people with him. Peter invited some of the
key disciples to come with him, and they went.

After fishing all night from a ship, they caught
nothing. Jesus uses this experience also to deal
with Peter:

> When the morning was now come, Jesus
> stood on the shore: but the disciples knew
> not that it was Jesus. Then Jesus saith unto
> them, Children....

John 21:4,5

The Greek word *paidion*,[1] used here to address
the disciples is not the usual word for children in

general. It refers to children who are under train-ing. When Jesus used it, it was as though He were saying, "Students, I'm about to teach you some-thing today." You may wonder why the disciples threw the net over, not knowing that it was Jesus telling them to do so.

The water is so clear in the Sea of Galilee that it is easy to see where the great schools of fish are located because they form dark shadows under the water. Sometimes men would stand on the hillside where they could see the dark shadows in the water, then yell at the fishermen in their boats and direct them to the schools of fish. If someone were to yell out from the shore, "Cast on the right side," the fishermen would think, *There's a school of fish over there.*

According to the Bible, the disciples did what Jesus said. They cast their net on the other side, and they were not able to draw it for the multi-tude of fishes. (v. 6.)

There were seven strong men in the boat—Simon, Thomas, Nathanael, the two sons of Zebedee, and two other disciples—and the catch was so big that they couldn't handle it.

Therefore that disciple whom Jesus loved saith unto Peter, "It is the Lord. Now when Simon Peter heard that it was the Lord, he girt his fisher's coat unto him (for he was naked,) and did cast himself into the sea" (v. 7).

Peter swam toward shore, while the other disciples came in a little boat taken from the larger fishing boat. They had a difficult time dragging in the net with the fish. There were only six of them left because Peter had jumped into the water.

As soon then as they were come to land, they saw a fire of coals there, and fish laid thereon, and bread. Jesus saith unto them, Bring of the fish, which ye have now caught…. Simon Peter went up, and drew the net to land full of great fishes, an hundred a fifty and three….

John 21:9-11

Peter could do what six men couldn't do before because he had seen Jesus. When we begin to get a vision of Jesus, the Bible says we can do all things through Christ Who strengthens us. (Phil. 4:13.) Peter began to receive the strength of Christ as soon as he saw Him, even though he had been in error again. He was running from his call, but he still pulled all those fish to the shore by himself. Once Peter pulls in the fish, Jesus dealt with him.

Notice that Jesus had built a fire. Peter had denied Jesus by a fire. When Peter saw that fire, he must have thought, *Oh, yes. I remember the last fire I was by with You, Jesus. I cursed then and denied You.*

Jesus wanted to show Peter something else by having that fire there: We don't have to camp by the enemy's fire. The Bible says that Jesus can set our hearts on fire. The two men who walked with Jesus on the road to Emmaus said later, "Did not our heart burn within us, while he talked with us by the way, and while he opened to us the scriptures?" (Luke 24:32).

Just be sure to get the right fire—the Holy Spirit, not the enemy's fire. The devil will burn you out; Jesus will give you a "holy heartburn." Jesus builds a fire that gives us boldness.

Instead of calling Peter into court and accusing him, saying, "Peter, you did this and this and this," Jesus had prepared breakfast for him. Notice that Jesus met Peter's physical needs first. Usually, we think the physical needs come last, but we see here that Jesus is very concerned about our physic needs.

After Jesus has met Peter's needs, He says to him, "Simon, son of Jonas...." Remember, when Jesus calls Peter. "Simon," He wants him to hear. He means, "Are you listening?" "...lovest thou me more than these?" (John 21:15).

In other words, Jesus was asking him, "Simon Peter, do you love Me more than you do this fishing trade?"

"Yes, Lord, You know I love You," Peter answers.

The word for love which Jesus uses here is *agape*: "Do you love Me with a love that gives and expects nothing back?"

When Peter answers, however, he uses a different word for love, *phileo*: "Lord, I said I would die for You. I said I wouldn't deny You, but I blew it. I don't love You with the kind of love that gives and expects nothing back."

Peter is so honest. He says, "I just love You with reciprocal love. You love me and I love You back. I love You like a friend."

Then Jesus says, "Feed my lambs" (v. 15). The word feed implies to give them food.[2] Notice that Jesus says "lambs," the little ones.

Again, Jesus says, "Simon, son of Jonas, lovest thou me?" (v. 16). "Do you love Me with agape love, a love that would die for Me?"

"Lord, You know how I love You," says Peter. "I love You with *phileo* love. Lord, You know that because You know me."

"Feed my sheep" (v. 16). A different word for feed is used here. It means "discipline and training." Jesus is saying, "Train My sheep." He also says "sheep," not "lambs," because you feed lambs, but you *train* sheep. "Feed My sheep—discipline them, educate them, train them."

Jesus says to Peter the third time, "Simon, son of Jonas, lovest thou me" (v. 17). But this time He uses the word *phileo:* "Do you even love Me with that kind of reciprocal love?"

Peter is grieved because Jesus asks him this question three times. He says to Jesus, "Do You doubt that I love You even with that kind of love? Lord, You know everything. You know that I do love You."

Again, Jesus says to Peter, "Feed my sheep" (v. 17). Here Jesus uses the word for feed which has the first meaning. He is saying, "Give My sheep the best nourishment you can give. Older sheep need to be fed as well as little lambs, and older sheep need to be trained."

Peter denied Jesus three times and Jesus asked Peter if he loves Him three times. Peter says, "I love You. I love You. I love You. I may not love You with the love I should, but I love You."

Finally, Jesus deals with the point at which Peter's fear began:

> Verily, verily, I say unto thee, When thou wast young, thou girdest thyself, and walkedst whither thou wouldest: but when thou shalt be old, thou shalt stretch forth thy hands, and another shall gird thee, and carry thee whither thou wouldest not.
>
> This spake he, signifying by what death he should glorify God. And when he had spoken this, he saith unto him, Follow me.
>
> John 21:18,19

Jesus was talking about death on the cross for Peter. According to history, this is the way Peter died. This type of death is pictured in the above passage, and Peter is the one who is frightened of crosses. Jesus is saying, "Peter, don't be afraid of the cross. You're going to die on one, too."

History records that when preparations were being made to crucify Peter, he said, "No, I'm not worthy to die like my Lord." So, at his own request, he was crucified upside down. Jesus took the fear out of Peter.

If someone said to me, "Marilyn, you're going to die on a cross," I would think, *Well, I'm never going to a foreign country to pass out tracts.* Wouldn't you? But Jesus delivered us from fear. We will be victorious anyway because we always triumph in Christ. (2 Cor. 2:14.)

Jesus is saying, "Peter, that cross you are so afraid of, that you don't want Me to go to . . . look, it's My resurrection. And, Peter, you're going to go to it, too; but you won't be worried about it or afraid. I'm taking you right to the cross—and out of it."

What a powerful deliverance from fear.

Then Peter, turning about, seeth the disciple whom Jesus loved following; which also leaned on his breast at supper, and said, Lord, which is he that betrayeth thee?

Peter seeing him saith to Jesus, Lord, and what shall this man do?

John 21:20,21

After reading this, we want to say, "Oh, Peter, don't you have enough to handle without wondering about everyone else?"

Jesus said, "Peter, just keep your eyes on Me. I'm going to take you through." (John 21:22.)

Not only has Jesus restored Peter from fear, forgiven him for his mistakes, gone to him and dealt with him directly, but He has brought him back into the ministry, which is where Peter should have been all along.

Jesus is saying, "Get out of fish, and get into sheep." At one time Jesus had said to Peter, "You'll fish for men." (Matt. 4:19.) But now He says, "You'll feed My sheep." (John 21:16,17.)

Peter was no longer afraid. But Peter, standing up with the eleven, lifted up his voice, and said unto them, "Ye men of Judea, and all ye that dwell at Jerusalem..."(Acts 2:14).

Peter then follows this introduction with a powerful sermon. This is the day of Pentecost—three thousand souls are converted this day. Peter could have been killed for his sermon. This is the Peter who has been restored from fear, the Peter who says, "It doesn't matter; I can go to the cross. I'm not afraid: Jesus is with me; He is in me." This is the Peter who could say with Paul, "I can do all things through Christ Who strengthens me."

Personality reactions are interesting—they reveal what a person is really like. Once Paul corrected Peter heavily by saying, "Peter, you wouldn't eat with the Gentile brethren; you got involved with dissimulation. You tried to act holier than the Gentile believers. You did wrong." (Gal. 2:14.)

But nowhere in either of Peter's epistles do we read that Peter was angry with Paul. Peter's old man was dead. Because he was already living in the cross, he was victorious. Even after being corrected by him, Peter referred to Paul as our beloved brother Paul (2 Pet. 3:15.)

In so many words, Peter was saying, "He was right; I was wrong, and I'm willing to admit it. I've been to the cross, and I'm dead anyway."

Dead men don't scream. Dead flesh doesn't scream. If our flesh is screaming, we haven't reckoned it dead at the cross. We are afraid of the cross, but the cross is the place of our victory. All our fears died 2,000 years ago on the cross.

What Jesus wants to say to us today is, "Are you a Simon? Are you a hearing one? Are you hearing what I'm saying to you?"

You may say, "Oh, I'm zealous." That's great. Be zealous, but be sure you are zealous in the Word.

Fear itself is a phobia. It's so ugly because it seems to possess a person and not let him go. That's why Jesus was always saying, "Don't be afraid. Fear not." When fear comes, we need to begin immediately to dismiss it.

Isaiah 26:3 says, "Thou wilt keep him in perfect peace, whose mind is stayed on thee: because he trusteth in thee." Jesus will keep us in peace; we don't have to worry.

Romans 8:15 says that we have not received the spirit of bondage. Fear is a bondage. We saw how Peter was bound by fear. Rather, we have received the Spirit of adoption whereby we can say, "Father, help me." And He will help.

Jesus didn't give us fear. Second Timothy 1:7 says, "For God hath not given us the sprit of fear; but of power, and of love, and of a sound mind." Psalm 34:4 says, "I sought the Lord, and he heard me, and delivered me from all my fears."

We don't have to be afraid when we hear the newscasters predict wars. Psalm 27:3 says, "Though an host should encamp against me, my heart shall not fear: though war should arise against me, in this will I be confident."

If any of us are afraid of the future, we shouldn't be – there is nothing to be afraid of. Psalm 112:7 says of the faithful man, "He shall not be afraid of evil tidings: his heart is fixed, trusting in the Lord." When we hear bad tidings, we should say immediately, "My heart is fixed. I'm trusting in the Lord. My heart is fixed on Him."

It's not good to be around people who are afraid because fear is contagious. Isaiah 8:12 says, "Neither fear ye their fear, nor be afraid." When we do have to be around people who are fearful, we need to remember 1 Peter 3:14 which says, "And be not afraid of their terror, neither be troubled."

Proverbs 28:1 tells us, "The wicked flee when no man pursueth: but the righteous are bold as a lion." Peter ran around like a chicken with its head cut off. He followed afar off and ran away when no one was even after him. The people were after Jesus, not Peter. That's an example of what fear does. But faith, the opposite of fear, makes us bold.

Let your flesh and fears die at the cross. Experience a resurrection of life, living with Jesus. When Jesus took Peter to the cross and delivered him, Peter was never afraid again. Let Jesus take you to the cross to deliver you from all your fears.

BANISH FEAR

I want to rebuke fear. Fear is the most hideous thing there is. "The fear of man bringeth a snare" (Prov. 29:25). Are you ready to get rid of fear? Put your hand on your heart and say this:

Satan, I curse you and any fear that you would bring upon me. You are the defeated one, and I am the victorious one.

You go around trying to plant bad seed in the earth, and the earth isn't even yours. The Bible says that the earth is the Lord's, and the fullness thereof. You come in to plant something that doesn't even belong to you, and you come in while men are asleep. But I'm not asleep; I'm awake. You're not planting anything in me because I am the Lord's, and He has planted His seed in me. That's good seed; it's the Word of God, and it can't return void.

I resist you in Jesus' name. I curse every attack of fear and every longstanding pattern of fear.

Father, I thank You, not only for wells bubbling up in me, but for rivers coming forth from me. In Jesus' name, amen.

Endnotes

Chapter 1

1 *International Standard Bible Encyclopedia,* Original James Orr 1915 Edition, Electronic Database. Copyright © 1995-1996 by Biblesoft. All rights reserved, s.v. "FEAR."

2 Ibid.

3 Ibid.

4 Ibid.

5 Based on a definition from Brown, Driver, Briggs and Gesenius, *The KJV Old Testament Hebrew Lexicon,* Hebrew Lexicon entry for "chared," <http://www. biblestudytools. .net/Lexicons/Hebrew/heb.cgi? number=2730&version=kjv>, s.v. "2730."

6 James Strong, "Greek Dictionary of the New Testament" in *Strong's Exhaustive Concordance of the Bible* (Nashville: Abingdon, 1890), p. 18, entry #870, s.v. "without fear," Luke 1:74.

Chapter 2

1 *International Standard Bible Encyclopedia,* s.v. "FEAR."

[2] Strong, p. 24, entry #1411, s.v. "virtue," Mark 5:30.

[3] *International Standard Bible Encyclopedia,* s.v. "POWER."

Chapter 6

[1] Strong, p. 54, entry #3813, s.v. "children," John 21:5.

[2] *MATTHEW HENRY'S COMMENTARY ON THE WHOLE BIBLE:* New Modern Edition, Electronic Database. Copyright 1991 by Hendrickson Publishers, Inc. John 21:15-19, "The divinity of Christ." Used by permission. All rights reserved.

About the Author

Marilyn Hickey is no stranger to impacting the lives of millions worldwide. As founder and president of Marilyn Hickey Ministries, Marilyn is being used by God to help "cover the earth with the Word." Her mission has been effectively accomplished through various avenues of ministry such as partnering with other ministries to ship thousands of Bibles into Communist countries; holding crusades in places like Ethiopia, the Philippines, Korea, Haiti, Brazil, Malaysia, Japan, and Honduras; and reaching individuals worldwide through television broadcasts seen on networks such as *Black Entertainment Network* (BET) and *Trinity Broadcasting Network* (TBN). In addition, Marilyn Hickey Ministries has established a fully accredited 2-year Bible college to raise up Christian leaders to carry out God's mission. Marilyn also serves the body of Christ as the Chairman of the Board of Regents for Oral Roberts University, and is the only woman serving on the Board of Directors for Dr. David Yonggi Cho (pastor of the world's largest congregation, Yoido Full Gospel Church.)

In addition to her ministry, Marilyn is also a busy wife and mother of two grown children. She is married to Wallace Hickey, pastor of Orchard Road Christian Center in Greenwood Village, Colorado.

Other Books by Marilyn Hickey

A Cry for Miracles

Angels All Around

Breaking Generational Curses

Devils, Demons and Deliverance

God's Covenant for Your Family

…He Will Give You Another Helper

How To Be a Mature Christian

Know Your Ministry

Maximize Your day

Names of God

Release the Power of the Blood Covenant

Satan-Proof Your Home

Signs in the Heavens

When Only a Miracle Will Do

Your Total Health Handbook:
Spirit, Soul and Body

Your Miracle Source

Beat Tension

Bold Men Win

Born-Again and Spirit-Filled

Bull Dog Faith

Change Your Life
Children Who Hit the Mark
Conquering Setbacks
Date To Be An Achiever
Don't Park Here
Experience Long Life
Fasting and Prayer
God's Benefit: Healing
Hold on to Your Dream
How To Win Friends
Keys to Healing Rejection
More Than a Conqueror
Power of Forgiveness
Power of the Blood
Receiving Resurrection Power
Renew Your Mind
Seven Keys to Make You Rich
Solving Life's Problems
Speak the Word
Stand in the Gap
Story of Esther
Tithes, Offerings, Alms
God's Plan for Blessing You!
Winning Over Weight
Women of the Word

Receive Jesus Christ
as Lord and Savior

The Bible says, "That if thou shalt confess with thy mouth the Lord Jesus, and shalt believe in thine heart that God hath raised him from the dead, thou shalt be saved. For with the heart man believeth unto righteousness; and with the mouth confession is made unto salvation" (Romans 10:9,10).

To receive Jesus Christ as Lord and Savior of your life, sincerely pray this prayer from your heart:

Dear Jesus,

I believe that You died for me and that You rose again on the third day. I confess to You that I am a sinner and that I need Your love and forgiveness. Come into my life, forgive my sins and give me eternal life. I confess You now as my Lord. Thank You for my salvation.

Signed_____ Dated _____

Write to us.
We will send you information to help you
with your new life in Christ.

Marilyn Hickey Ministries · P.O. Box 17340
Denver, CO 80217 · (303) 770-0400

Or visit us on the Web:
www.mhmin.org

Prayer Requests

Let us join our faith with yours for your prayer needs.
Fill out below and send to:

Marilyn Hickey Ministries
P.O. Box 17340
Denver, CO 80217

Prayer request _____

_____

_____

Mr. & Mrs. ☐   Mr. ☐   Miss ☐

Name _____

Address _____

City _____

State_____ Zip _____

Home Phone (_____) _____

Work Phone (_____) _____

Call for prayer TOLL-FREE, 24-hours a day
1-877-661-1249.

Or leave your prayer request
at our website/ministry center:
www.mhmin.org

WORD TO THE
WORLD COLLEGE

Explore your options and increase your knowledge of the Word at this unique college of higher learning for men and women of faith. Word to the World College **offers on-campus and correspondence courses** that give you the opportunity to learn from Marilyn Hickey and other great Bible scholars, who can help prepare you to be an effective minister of the gospel. Classes are available for both full- and part-time students.

For more information, complete the coupon below and send to:

Word to the World College
P.O. Box 17340
Denver, CO 80217
(303)770-0400

Mr. & Mrs. ☐   Mr. ☐   Miss ☐

Name _____

Address _____

City _____

State_____ Zip _____

Home Phone (_____) _____

Work Phone (_____) _____

Or contact us on the Web: www.mhmin.org

For Your Information
Free Monthly Magazine

Please send me your free monthly magazine OUT-POURING (including daily devotionals, timely articles, and ministry updates)!

Tapes and Books

Please send me Marilyn's latest product catalog:

Mr. & Mrs. ☐   Mr. ☐   Miss ☐

Name _____

Address _____

City _____

State_____ Zip _____

Home Phone (_____) _____

Work Phone (_____) _____

Mail to:
Marilyn Hickey Ministries
P.O. box 17340
Denver, CO 80217
(303) 770-0400

Touching You

With the Love of

Jesus!

Marilyn Hickey

PRAYER CENTER

When was the last time that you could say, "He touched me right where I hurt"? No matter how serious the nature of your call, we're here to pray the Word and show you how to touch Jesus for real answers to real problems.

Call us and let's touch Jesus, together!

Call for prayer TOLL-FREE, 24-hours a day:

1-877-661-1249

WE CARE!

Additional copies of this book
Are available from your local bookstore.

Harrison House
Tulsa, Oklahoma 74153

The Harrison House Vision

Proclaiming the truth and the power
Of the Gospel of Jesus Christ
With excellence;

Challenging Christians to
Live victoriously,
Grow spiritually,
Know God intimately.